ROOTS
of
HAPPINESS

To Lucy and Thea,
may you find as many moments of happiness
as you have given me.

S. D.

For Steph,
whose friendship has brought me
happiness for as long as I can remember.

H. H.

PUFFIN BOOKS

UK | USA | Canada | Ireland | Australia
India | New Zealand | South Africa

Puffin Books is part of the Penguin Random House group of companies
whose addresses can be found at global.penguinrandomhouse.com.

www.penguin.co.uk   www.puffin.co.uk   www.ladybird.co.uk

Penguin
Random House
UK

First published 2023

001

Text copyright © Susie Dent, 2023
Illustrations copyright © Harriet Hobday, 2023

The moral right of the author and illustrator has been asserted

Text design by Sally Griffin
Printed and bound in China

The authorized representative in the EEA is Penguin Random House Ireland,
Morrison Chambers, 32 Nassau Street, Dublin D02 YH68

A CIP catalogue record for this book is available from the British Library

ISBN: 978-0-241-57319-8

All correspondence to:
Puffin Books, Penguin Random House Children's
One Embassy Gardens, 8 Viaduct Gardens
London, SW11 7BW

ROOTS
of
HAPPINESS

100 WORDS FOR JOY AND HOPE
FROM BRITAIN'S MOST-LOVED WORD EXPERT

SUSIE DENT

illustrated by Harriet Hobday

PUFFIN

INTRODUCTION

In my job, I spend a lot of time with dictionaries, studying the stories behind the words in each of their pages. I feel very lucky because every day I discover new, exciting words and learn more about the incredible power of language. But I have also noticed how much our language focuses on negative things. We have so many words for sad thoughts and emotions, which means it is much easier for us to moan rather than to celebrate. In fact, many more positive words did once exist, but they have been left behind over the centuries, and others have been forgotten altogether. Did you know, for example, that you could once be 'ruthful', which means 'full of compassion', as well as ruth*less*? Or that you could be 'ept' as well as 'inept', and even full of 'gorm' (care and attention) rather than just 'gormless'?

I'm on a mission to bring these 'lost' positive words back into our lives, and would love your help to do it. Because research has proven that by having the words to describe happy feelings, we can *feel* that happiness directly. Which means that language has incredible power, for not only can it describe how we feel, it can even *change* those feelings. So if you are feeling a little sad or blue, try focusing on one of the words from this book, such as 'plodge' (page 68), 'dumbledore' (page 67), or 'scurryfunge' (page 92). If you do, you might bring some sparkle to a gloomy day, and maybe even a smile to other people's faces too. I would love *Roots of Happiness* to give you lots of magical moments just like this.

Two thousand years ago, the Roman emperor Marcus Aurelius gave some good advice: 'Dwell on the beauty of life,' he said. 'Watch the stars, and see yourself running with them.' His message was to focus on the things that make us happy, and on the beauty in our lives that we sometimes overlook. Think of special moments, like watching snowflakes as they begin to fall, hearing the whispering of trees in a summer breeze, feeling the build-up to Christmas, or seeing a butterfly flutter past your window. There are words to describe each of these moments, and they themselves can make us smile.

What do *you* think of when you hear the word 'happy'? Does it take you back to a single event in time when everything seemed perfect? Perhaps it's something you associate with the people or animals in your life. Or it might be exactly how you're feeling now, as you sit down to read a book. Wherever you find it, we'd all agree that happiness is a feeling to treasure, particularly because none of us are happy *all* the time. We are all familiar with sadness and stress, and so happiness feels all the more special when it comes. What better way to celebrate it than through words – ones that remind us of the joyful things in life that we can cherish? This is what *Roots of Happiness* is all about.

I have selected one hundred words that I hope will make you smile, and will help you bring happiness to others too. You will see that the words in the book are arranged chronologically, appearing in the order in which they were first used, and with a pronunciation guide at the back of the book. We start with the oldest – 'good' – which was first used over a thousand years ago, and travel through time, uncovering other lesser-known joyful words too.
But language is always evolving, and it's not only these long-forgotten words that I will explore. We finish with some words from recent times that you might know, such as 'FOMO' or 'amazeballs', and some you might not, like 'snaccident', which describes the accidental eating of an entire packet of biscuits when you meant to have just the one!

I chose each of the hundred words because they make *me* happy – some because I love their sound (who can resist a smile when they hear the word 'cacklefart'?) and others because they have a lovely and secret history. Take the expression 'lick something into shape', for example, and discover its wonderful story on page 24.

There are many secret stories like this that I'd love to introduce you to, as well as words you will never have heard before. Ones like 'mubble-fubbles', which actually describes the state of being down in the dumps, but just sounds so cuddly and reassuring that you can't help but smile. Or words like 'apricity' and 'gossamer', which describe beautiful splashes of magic in nature.

There are words from other languages too, because however rich the
English language is, there will always be some gaps we haven't yet filled.
In these pages you will find Turkish words, Hebrew words, a word from the
Philippines that means the 'irresistible desire to squeeze something cute',
and many more!

You can read *Roots of Happiness* in lots of different ways: by dipping into it
from time to time as a pick-me-up, or by starting at the beginning and
reading right through! It's up to you to choose, for this is your book, and its
words are yours. Nor does it matter what age you are: whether you are 5 or
100, this collection is meant for anyone and everyone who needs some
word-drops of magic and joy in their life.

Marcus Aurelius was right – let's dwell on the beauty of life and run with the
stars, by focusing on the things that make us happy. For me, words are the
greatest of all those things. I would love it if, after reading *Roots of Happiness*,
you feel the same way too.

Susie Dent

GOOD

'Good' is one of the oldest words in the English language, and it has been a positive word from the start. It began with an ancient word 'goda', meaning 'fitting together'. So now, when we say 'life is good', we are really saying that everything is fitting together nicely, in perfect harmony.

Today, 'good' is one of the top one thousand words we use most often. You might say 'that's a good film' or 'this food tastes good', tell someone 'it's good to see you', or tell your dog she's 'such a good girl'. All of these describe something or someone who is pleasing or welcome.

There is a curious fact about 'good' – we have never used 'gooder' or 'goodest' to mean 'more good' or 'most good', as you might expect. Instead, we use 'better' and 'best'. The same thing happens in other languages, but no one has yet discovered why!

LOVEWENDE

Who do you think of when you hear the word 'love'?

'Love' means a deep affection for something or for someone. This wonderful emotion comes in many different forms, whether that's the feelings we hold for our family, our pets, or even a passion or hobby. In the past, 'love' came with lots of different word-companions. A 'love-glance', for example, was a loving look between two people, while a 'love-spoon' was a decorated wooden spoon, presented by a man to the person he wanted to marry. And then there is 'lovewende', a word that has now disappeared but that describes a person who is both loving to others, and loved deeply in return.

The word 'love' is very old, yet a thousand years on, our language has no other word that means exactly the same thing. Sadly, there are far more words in the dictionary for 'hate' than there are for 'love'. Wouldn't it be nice to bring back some of these joyful expressions from the past?

DARLING

What words do your loved ones use when they talk
to you? 'Poppet' perhaps? Or 'sweetheart'? They might also
use 'darling', which has been a term of affection for over
a thousand years. 'Darling' literally means 'little dear', and
is one of many words used for someone we love. Some,
from the past, will sound very strange to us now:
'bagpudding', for example, or 'cabbage', 'flittermouse'
(an old term for a bat) or 'ding-ding'!

TREE

Although they mean different things, 'tree' and 'true' probably come from the same family. Both come from an ancient root meaning 'firm' and 'solid'. Trees have been symbols of faithfulness for centuries, because they stand stable and upright in the earth and can withstand stormy weather. The oldest tree in existence is thought to be almost 5,000 years old! In the same way, a 'true' friend is faithful and loyal, as strong and enduring as an oak tree.

The German-Swiss writer and poet Hermann Hesse once said:

'Trees are sanctuaries.
When we have learned to listen
to trees... that is home.
That is happiness.'

FREOND-SPEDIG

*'A day without a friend is like a pot without
a single drop of honey left inside.'*
WINNIE THE POOH

Friends make the world a better place. From its very beginnings
in the 8th century, the word 'friend' has meant the same thing:
someone who is valued and trusted.

Alongside the delightful characters Eeyore and Piglet, together with
Kanga, Roo, Owl, Rabbit and Tigger, Pooh could be described as
'freond-spedig', meaning 'rich in friends'. *Freond* was the oldest
spelling of the word 'friend', while *spedig* meant 'wealthy'.

They may not look very similar now, but the words 'free' and 'friend'
are from the same family. They both come from an ancient word
meaning 'dearly loved'. In ancient times, members of a household
who were considered family, and not working as slaves or
servants, were thought to be 'free' and within the
circle of love and friendship.

BUTTERFLY

Picture a hazy, dozy summer's day, with a table set for
lunch outside. Perhaps you can see a beautiful butterfly
with blazing colours, gently fluttering on to a plate? If so,
you might be close to solving the mystery of how one
of our most treasured insects was named.

We have been using the word 'butterfly' for over a
thousand years, and people have been trying to work out
the origin of its name ever since. Could it be because many
common butterflies have pale yellow wings, like butter?
Or perhaps it comes from the belief that butterflies really do
love butter and often land on any that has been left out, just
like on that lunch table in your imagination! Some people
even believe that 'butterfly' began as 'flutterby' because
of the way the insects gracefully flutter by us as
they fly through the sky.

We also think of these creatures when we are
a little bit nervous or excited about something,
and we use the phrase 'I have butterflies'. This
perfectly captures those moments where it
feels like there are tiny wings fluttering
away in our stomachs!

DOG

Dogs have been our favourite companions for a very long time.
But before we loved 'dogs' we loved 'hounds', for this was the word
that people used for the animal a thousand years ago. Where 'dog'
came from is a bit of a mystery, but we do know that the earliest
records of the word appear in surnames of people living in the 13th
century, including Richard Doggetail and Roger Le Doge!

The names of individual dog breeds are less puzzling. Some are
based on the country they originated from – an Alsatian, for example,
comes from the French region of Alsace. Other names come from
the habits of the breed – 'poodle' comes from the German
Pudelhund – 'splash-hound' – because poodles
are water dogs and love splashing about.

The 'terrier' is named after the French for 'earth',

because these dogs love to

burrow in the earth

or terrain.

ZEPHYR

Imagine the feeling of lying on the grass on a
hot day, staring up at the sky and enjoying the
warmth of the Sun on your face. If you're lucky, as
the summer heat beats down, a gentle breeze
might waft over your skin. This joyous sensation is
a 'zephyr', a beautiful old word for a very light
wind. For the Ancient Greeks, Zephyrus was the
god of the west wind, whose sweet breath was
said to blow gently across the Earth.

Say 'zephyr' softly out loud. Don't you think the sound perfectly suits a pleasant breeze on a summer's day?

GORM

No one ever wants to be called 'gormless', which means
clumsy or careless. Instead, wouldn't it be lovely to be told that
you are 'gormful'? Centuries ago, this would have meant you took
great care over things, and to be 'gorm-like' was to have an
intelligent look about you! The word 'gorm' came into English from
Old Norse, the language of the Viking invaders, almost 1,200
years ago. Why not find a friend or family member who is
caring and intelligent and let them know
how gormful they are!

RUTH

Do you know anyone named Ruth? If you do, you can tell them
that their name means 'full of compassion'. To 'have ruth' in the 13th century
meant to feel sorrow and pity for another person. Today, we have lost this
positive word and remember only its unpleasant sibling 'ruthless', which means
having no compassion at all. Perhaps we should bring back the lost 'ruthful'
and use it to describe people who are kind and look out for others.

In fact, there are lots of similarly positive words that have disappeared.
Long ago, we could be 'ruly' if we followed the rules, but today we only
remember 'unruly', meaning naughty or disruptive.

CHEER

'Cheer' is happiness, optimism and confidence. When we cheer someone on, we shout in encouragement.

INWIT

Your conscience is the knowledge or feeling, deep inside, that urges you to be kind and good. 'Inwit' was once the name for this inner knowledge. Your inwit might tell you not to steal, for example, or to be caring towards another person.

While your inwit was deeply personal, your 'outwit', on the other hand, described the way you saw and understood the world. Both come from the word 'wit', which originally meant intelligence and understanding. To 'wit' something was to know it. We don't use 'inwit' or 'outwit' any more, but we do still use 'wit' on its own to mean quick thinking, and a talent for saying clever or funny things. A 'nitwit', meanwhile, doesn't show much understanding at all!

FLOTHER

Snowballs, snowmen, sledging and steaming cups
of hot chocolate – we all love snowy days, don't we?
We may not experience as many of them as we would like,
but we do have a surprising number of words that we can
use in gloriously snowy weather. A 'flother', for example, is a
single flake of snow that suggests more are on their way. So
when you see a 'flother', you can really start to feel excited!

The Scots know all about snow and have a very big
vocabulary for it. A light snow shower, for example,
is a 'flindrikin', while 'feefling' describes snow
as it swirls above our heads in the chilly air.

GOSSAMER

Imagine looking out of your window on a cold November morning. Can you picture tiny white threads floating in the air or draped over grass, branches and bushes? These threads can look quite enchanting, and they are known as 'gossamer'. This delicate substance is actually made up of very fine cobwebs spun by tiny, crafty spiders!

The word 'gossamer' first appeared in the 14th century. It is probably short for 'goose summer', because geese were once traditionally hunted in the autumn and winter months, when gossamer is usually seen. Others think that the fine, silky material was named after geese because the downy threads look as though they are made of goose feathers.

So next time you see those soft white threads floating in the air, you can call them by their name 'gossamer' and thank them for bringing a little touch of magic to a chilly winter's day.

TICKLE

We can't help but laugh when we're being
tickled, and there's something about the sound
of 'tickle' that brings a smile too. The word has
described a thrill of pleasure for over 600 years.
We can be tickled by a thought, and we
can of course be tickled by a touch.
And if we are really delighted by
something, then we can say
we are
'tickled
pink'!

KITTEN

Kittens take their name from an old French word *chaton*, meaning 'little cat'. We have been using the word 'kitten' for baby cats for over 600 years.

ELIXIR

If you could make a magic potion, what would you like it to do? Perhaps it could make you invisible, or give you wings so you could fly? In ancient times, people believed that magical potions really existed, and they called them 'elixirs'. These liquids all came in different forms and were believed to make extraordinary things happen. The 'elixir of life' made people immortal, while another could change ordinary metals into gold.

The people who made these potions were called alchemists, and they were believed to have the power to transform things as if by magic. Over the centuries, they began to use more scientific methods, and became known simply as chemists. Today, when we study chemistry, we might not create magic mixtures, but we are building upon beliefs from thousands of years ago.

HAPPY

To be happy is to be joyous,
glad or pleased.

HALCYON

Have you ever been lucky enough to see a kingfisher?
Perhaps you've seen photos or paintings of one, with its startling
colours of orange and sky-blue. Kingfishers are special birds, not
just because of their striking appearance, but because for a long
time they were associated with magic. The Ancient Greeks
believed that kingfishers made their nests upon the sea,
while the gods of the wind made sure the water stayed
totally calm. The ancient name for this beautiful
bird was 'halcyon', and today we use the
expression 'halcyon days' to mean days
of happiness, when everything
is still and peaceful.

DEWLAP

An animal's 'dewlaps' are the floppy folds of skin around its mouth that bounce up and down as it runs!

MUSCLE

'Muscle' seems quite an ordinary word, but the story behind it will definitely make you smile. The muscles in our body are responsible for every move we make. We have about 650 of them, all working together as a team to keep us moving! If you exercise or play sport regularly, your muscles will become stronger and more visible. The word 'muscle' comes from Latin, the language spoken by the Ancient Romans. When they saw an athlete flexing their arm, they imagined the moving muscle was a tiny rodent scurrying about under the skin. And so they gave the biceps the name *musculus*, which means 'little mouse'! *Musculus* eventually became 'muscle' in English, meaning the story of the tiny mouse was long forgotten . . .

FORBLISSED

Think back to a time when you have been really, really happy.
Maybe you're remembering a moment when you were
surrounded by people and everyone was full of laughter.
Or perhaps you're thinking of a time when you were alone,
peaceful, quiet and content. Centuries ago, such a feeling might
have been described as being 'forblissed'. 'Bliss' is another word
for 'joy', and so to be 'forblissed' is to be extremely happy.

Long ago, people would often use 'for-' in front of a word to
describe a particular state or mood. To be 'forwearied' was to be
very tired, to be 'foridled' was to be feeling very lazy, and to be
'forswunk' was to be exhausted from too much work!
'Forblissed' is definitely the happiest of them all.

CORDIAL

If you enjoy a glass of orange squash, you might know that another name for 'squash' is 'cordial'. So it might seem strange to discover that 'cordial' actually means 'from the heart'. What does a fruit drink have to do with the heart? Well, these drinks were first used as medicine, designed to cure illnesses and to keep people's hearts healthy and strong.

We also use 'cordial' another way, as an adjective meaning 'friendly' and 'warm'. And that comes back to the heart once again, because when we are cordial towards someone, our affection is 'heartfelt'.

LICK INTO SHAPE

Centuries ago, it was believed by many, including the playwright William Shakespeare, that bear cubs were born as blobs without any shape at all. That's when their mothers would come along. People thought that the mother bears would physically lick their cubs into a bear shape, with fluffy ears, a pointy snout and a warm, fuzzy coat. This strange but beautiful belief lasted for hundreds of years, but its story has now been lost in time.

But the phrase hasn't been lost! Has anyone ever told you to get something in order by 'licking' it 'into shape'? Although licking has nothing to do with tidying a room or getting your homework done, when today someone asks you to 'lick something into shape', they might not realize the secret story behind the expression, which is all about a mother's love for her children.

CHARM

You can have a lot of fun with what are known as 'collective nouns' – words used to describe a group or collection of things. Many of them we already know – a 'gang of thieves', for example, or a 'bunch of grapes'. But what would you call a group of witches? A cackler, perhaps? How about a collection of Lego pieces – might that be a 'foot-hurt'?

A lot of collective nouns refer to animals and birds. You might find a 'pride of lions' prowling across the savannah, or a 'pod of dolphins' swimming through the ocean. If you're really lucky, you might have even seen a 'murmuration of starlings', which describes a group of hundreds of birds

that twist, turn and swoop together, making beautiful swirling patterns in the sky.

A 'charm' is another collective noun, this time for the goldfinch –
a beautiful, bright yellow bird. The word for a group of these birds
makes perfect sense, as there's something quite magical and
charming about their golden feathers.

27

MATUTINAL

Are you someone who jumps out of bed in the morning, excited to face the new day? If you are the type of person who loves early mornings and feels cheery and energetic, then you are 'matutinal'.

SUSPIRE

Do you remember a time when you felt very nervous or stressed? Hopefully everything actually turned out OK, and when it was over, you could breathe a big sigh of relief. Long ago, that sighing would have been known as 'suspiring', a word that meant simply letting out a deep breath, especially one of happiness or relief.

'Suspire' comes from the Latin *spirare*, meaning 'to breathe'. There are many other English words to do with breathing that are part of the same family tree. To 'inspire' someone is to 'breathe' life into their ideas, and when we 'perspire' we 'breathe out' moisture through our skin.

MELLIFLUOUS

Certain noises, sounds, voices and words are particularly lovely and satisfying to hear. Try saying:

'lollipop',

'sunshine',

'bumblebee',

'hush'

or
'giggle'.

There is a word to describe such sweet and soothing sounds – 'mellifluous'. At the heart of this word is pure sweetness, for the Latin *mel* means 'honey', and *fluere* means 'flow'. So 'mellifluous' describes sounds and words that are so mellow they 'flow like honey'.

AURORA

Imagine standing beside a frozen lake in Alaska, looking up at the night sky and gazing at thousands of twinkling stars. Suddenly you notice splashes of pink, green or yellow appearing and getting larger and larger, until soon the whole sky is lit up with magical, swirling colours. This spectacular light show is known as the Northern Lights. It is caused by tiny particles crashing into our atmosphere and forming an explosion of colour, also known as the *aurora borealis*, the 'northern aurora'.

3,000 years ago, in Greek and Roman mythology, Aurora was the goddess of the dawn. She was believed to race across the sky each morning in a multicoloured chariot, announcing the arrival of the Sun and the start of a new day. Today, we also use 'aurora' to mean the dawn.

RESPAIR

Most of us know the word 'despair', a word that describes
deep unhappiness and a loss of hope, but did you know that
there once was a word to describe the opposite? 'Respair',
from the 16th century, expresses something quite joyful: fresh
hope and a recovery from despair. It is a word and a feeling to
hang on to when things seem a little sad. In difficult times, it is
good to remember that the sadness will pass,
and respair will eventually find you.

PANACEA

Wouldn't it be nice to have a cure for every disease
and difficulty? Well, the Ancient Greeks believed that such
a magical cure existed, and they called it a 'panacea'. They
borrowed this name from the Greek goddess of healing,
who was thought to have the power to cure any human
illness and to relieve people from all distress. Her name,
Panacea, came from the Greek *pan*, meaning 'all', and *akos*,
meaning 'remedy' or 'medicine'.

Pan pops up in other words too. A 'pantomime'
originally involved an actor who mimed all the parts
in a play. A 'panorama' is a picture showing
an entire scene or landscape.

CWTCH

Is there anything nicer than a hug? Hugs have been scientifically proven to make us feel better, warmer, comforted and more loved. There is even an International Hugging Day every year to celebrate them across the world!

Some linguists believe that the word 'hug' was left to us by the Vikings, who invaded British shores between the 8th and 11th centuries. They had a reputation for being violent plunderers and pillagers, so there is something rather sweet in the fact that they gave us our word for a hug. Many other words from their language of Old Norse settled in English too, including 'husband', 'freckle', 'give', 'take', 'get', 'cake' and 'egg'. 'Hug' probably began with the Old Norse *hygge*, meaning to comfort.

In Welsh, there is a special word for a hug, which is 'cwtch'. A 'cwtch' means a safe place of belonging. It originally meant a tiny space or cubbyhole, before becoming a word for the cosy and comforting feeling of a warm embrace.

BELLYCHEER

We all have a favourite comfort food: a snack or
meal that we look forward to the most, or that cheers us
up when we're feeling down. For some it might be a roast
dinner, while for others it might be Saturday morning
pancakes with lots of maple syrup.

In the 16th century, they knew comfort food as 'bellycheer',
because of the way it cheered up their stomachs!

On the other hand, the food they ate to
stay full and healthy was known at that time
as 'belly-timber' – like a tree or strong piece
of wood, it kept them propped up!

FIZZLE

Farts, trouser burps, pumps or trumps – whatever you call them, 'fizzle' probably isn't on your list! Yet the very first meaning of this word was 'to break wind quietly'. A long time ago, people must have thought of this when they heard a feeble hissing noise, which is why we now use 'fizzle' to describe something such as a flame that quietly splutters and then goes out. Just like a windipop!

MUBBLE-FUBBLES

The end of summer, Sunday evenings, falling out with a friend – moments like these can leave us feeling a little sad or down in the dumps. People have experienced these emotions for hundreds of years, and in the 16th century there was quite a playful way of describing them: the 'mubble-fubbles'. No one quite knows where the expression comes from, but if you try saying it out loud, you might find that it makes you smile – just what we need if we are feeling down!

The dictionary has quite a few other words to express the same feelings, and all of them are just as fun to say aloud. Next time you feel a bit low you can always say you have the 'woofits', the 'blahs', the 'glumps' or the 'humdrums', and see if it lifts your spirits!

LULLABY

Lullabies are quiet, gentle bedtime songs
that are sung to send children to sleep. The
word 'lullaby' is almost as soothing as the
songs themselves, don't you think? At its
heart is the word 'lull', which means to
calm or soothe, and 'bye', a word that you
will often find in lullabies themselves,
such as 'Rock-a-bye Baby'.

'Twinkle twinkle little star,
how I wonder what you are . . .'

DORMOUSE

A dormouse is a tiny mouse-like rodent with a bushy tail, long whiskers and big, round eyes. You might think its name is a little bit odd, but in fact the 'dor' has nothing to do with doors and everything to do with dozing! The name of this charming little animal is based on the French *dormir*, meaning 'to sleep'. It was chosen by naturalists because the dormouse is a sleepy creature that likes to hibernate between the autumn and spring. It makes a nest deep in a hedge or on the ground, and lines it with soft material such as grass or leaves. It then curls up into a tight ball and goes to sleep all through the winter.

41

MEANDER

In ancient times, a certain river, named after the river god Maeander, was celebrated for its long and winding course. It turned this way and that as it flowed through a region called Ionia until it reached the Aegean Sea. This river still flows today in south-western Turkey, and is now called the Büyük Menderes River.

The Maeander River was so well known that 'meandering' became a word in English for wandering aimlessly or for following a winding course. And the word can truly bring feelings of calm and serenity, as you picture yourself meandering across a field on a lazy summer's day.

FELLOWFEELING

When things go wrong for someone we
care about, or when we witness another person's
unhappiness, we feel compassion. This word means
sympathy, pity and concern, and comes from the
Latin for 'suffering with', because we share in
other people's unhappiness.

Hundreds of years ago, sharing in the feelings
of those we love or care about was also known as
'fellowfeeling'. It is a profoundly positive emotion
and is part of what makes us human.

SPINDRIFT

Imagine walking along a beach on a blustery day, watching the waves curl as they come into shore. Can you almost taste the salty tang of the ocean? The droplets of water that carry that taste go by the beautiful name of 'spindrift' – spray blown up by the wind from the crests of the waves.

CONFELICITY

Confelicity is the joy we feel in seeing another person's happiness. From con, meaning 'with' and *felicitas* (Latin), meaning 'happiness'.

HAPPIFY

Happiness is a wonderful feeling. And making other people happy can also make you feel great. There are so many things you can do to bring happiness to yourself or to others. Whether it's listening to your favourite music, spending time doing things you love, or doing something kind for someone else, little actions can lift your spirits and make you and the people you know smile.

Wouldn't it be good if we had a single word to express this? It turns out we actually do, even if most of us don't know it. In the 17th century, to 'happify' meant to please the heart and fill people with happiness.

ERUMPENT

The season of spring is a special time of growth
and new beginnings. It is when leaves appear on the
trees and flowers come into bloom. This period was
once known more fully as 'the spring of the leaf'. One
word that describes the new growth that springs up
all around us is 'erumpent', meaning 'bursting out'.
When you say the world aloud, you can almost
hear that sudden explosion into bud and
leaf, don't you think?

APRICITY

It's freezing outside, frost is blanketing the ground, and the world seems icily quiet and still. Stepping into such a landscape might well make you shiver and hunch your shoulders. Imagine, then, how wonderful it would feel if the sunshine broke through the mist and shed its warmth upon you. There is a beautiful word for this joyful sensation of sunshine on a winter's day: 'apricity', which sounds almost as beautiful as the feeling itself. It is related to a similar word, 'apricate', meaning to bask in sunshine.

Just a single printed record of 'apricity' has been found since it first appeared in the 17th century. Wouldn't it be wonderful to bring this word back into our language?

The joy of apricity in winter is very hard to beat.

NIVEOUS

Niveous describes snow that is so startlingly
white it's as if it's shimmering under the
light of the Sun or the Moon.

SEIJAKU

Life can be very noisy sometimes, both on our screens and in the world around us. Quiet moments of peace can be precious, and the Japanese language has a word for such times of serenity and stillness: 'seijaku'. It describes a moment of healing that can be found particularly in nature, when we stop and breathe for a little while.

FRIENDED

People have always liked to try out new word inventions
and to play around with existing words to create new ones.
One adventurous way of creating new language is to turn
nouns and adjectives into verbs – it sounds complicated, but
it's what we do when we 'nose around' for ideas, 'hand in'
our work, or if something 'weirds us out'.

The great playwright William Shakespeare liked to play
with language too. He used the word 'friended', for example,
to mean 'make friends with', and wrote lines such as 'grace
me no grace, nor uncle me no uncle', even turning 'uncle'
into a verb! Language is always changing – and you could
create your own new words this way too. Perhaps you
might be 'biscuiting' as you read this!

SCINTILLATE

Tinsel sparkling beneath the fairy lights. The flickers of a firework as it falls from the sky. The glint from a diamond as it catches the beams of the Sun. Small flashes of light can look quite wondrous. One word for these sparkling objects is 'scintillating', which can describe both the twinkling of stars in the night sky and the glimmer of objects such as cut glass or fire. The word is built upon the Latin *scintillare*, meaning to sparkle or glitter.

The word can also be used for someone's personality or company. If someone is dazzling and brilliant, they may be described as scintillating.

LAGOM

In the fairy tale of Goldilocks and the Three Bears, the young girl Goldilocks, tired and hungry, enters the forest home of a family of bears. Spotting three bowls of porridge laid out on a table, she decides to eat from one. The first is too hot, and the second is too cold, but the third is just right. Goldilocks then lies down on the big bed and says, 'This bed is too hard!' She tries out the medium bed and cries, 'This bed is too soft!' Finally, she lies down on the small bed and declares, 'This bed is just right', before falling asleep.

In Swedish, there is a word for something that is not too much, and not too little, but just right – *lagom*. Next time you try a mattress that is neither too hard nor too soft, a pair of jeans that is neither too baggy nor too tight, or a film that is neither too long nor too short, you can talk about this perfection by describing it as 'lagom'.

VERMICELLI

Italy is the home of pasta. From spaghetti to penne, farfalle to rigatoni, there are many different types of this delicious food, and their names often mean something quite fun and surprising.

Think of a steaming bowl of spaghetti – what do you see? Perhaps a collection of little strings? The Italians must have thought that too, because 'spaghetti' means exactly that.

The shape of 'penne', meanwhile, must have reminded people of 'pens' or 'feathers' (early pens were feathers dipped in ink, known as 'quills').

'Cannelloni', rolls of pasta stuffed with meat or vegetables, means 'large tubes', while the curly 'farfalle' shape means 'butterfly'.

Perhaps the strangest of them all, however, is 'vermicelli', which looks like long and slender threads. The name of this pasta means 'little worms'!

CERULEAN

Golden sands stretching for miles along the shore of a deep blue sea – it's the scene of a picture postcard. In fact, the sea can take on many colours as light bounces off it, from greens to blues and even black, but most of us see it in our minds as an exquisite blue – just as blue as the sky above it.

There is a word for this beautiful colour: 'cerulean', which was borrowed from the Latin *caelum*, meaning 'sky'. 'Cerulean' has been used by poets since the 17th century to describe the deep blue depths of the ocean, or the azure colour of a cloudless sky.

DIMPSY

'It's getting a bit dimpsy' is a sentence you might
hear in Devon or Cornwall, in the south-west of Britain.
'Dimpsy' is one of thousands of regional words that
have stayed local to the areas they came from. Meaning
'dusky', it refers to the twilight that accompanies the
setting of the Sun. The word is used when the natural
light of day is dimming and it will soon be dark.

The word 'twilight' is just as beautiful, as it is based
on an old version of the word 'two', and refers to
the light we see in the sky as the day hovers
between two states – day and night.

For a while dusk was also called the
'twitter-light', perhaps as a reference to
the soft twittering or chirruping of
the birds as dusk falls.

HIBERNACLE

Have you ever made a cosy den at home or in the garden – a secret place you can hide away in and feel safe and relaxed? Animals do this too, particularly in winter, when small mammals like hedgehogs, tortoises, squirrels and dormice hibernate until spring appears. The hideaway that these animals choose is known as a 'hibernacle', which comes from a Latin word *hibernus*, meaning 'wintery'. A hibernacle is an animal's winter hideout, one that is warm and safe. Next time we curl up in a secret haven, just like squirrels and hedgehogs in gardens, we could call it our 'hibernacle' too!

CACKLEFART

There are lots of ways to serve eggs –
scrambled or poached on toast, boiled and served
with soldiers, or fried with sausages and bacon. But
would these meals sound quite so delicious if the
eggs were called 'cacklefarts'?! It might sound silly,
but this was a popular and playful word for an egg a
hundred years ago. The word conjures up the funny
image of a cackling hen squeezing out an egg.

And while you're enjoying your egg, how about
adding some 'bags of mystery'? This was another
tongue-in-cheek expression, used this time to
describe sausages – the Victorians decided that
sausages are full of mystery because you
never quite know what's in them!

GLAMOUR

What do you think of when you hear the word 'glamorous'? Do you picture film stars walking up the red carpet, cameras flashing all around? Or perhaps you think of someone wearing a gorgeous outfit and exotic jewellery? One thing that you're probably not imagining is a book on grammar! Yet that is exactly how the word 'glamour' began, as 'grammar' and 'glamour' are siblings from the same family, and both were once very magical.

Their story began in medieval times, when 'grammar' meant every subject of learning. Education in those times included astrology (the study of the stars and the supernatural world), which is how 'grammar' became associated with magic. Centuries later, the word 'glamour' was invented as a spin-off from 'grammar' to take on its magical or charming side. 'Grammar', meanwhile, began to focus on education, and in particular the study of language.

This means that anyone who loves exploring languages is really *very* glamorous – or perhaps we should say 'grammarous'!

SERENDIPITY

There once was a story about three princes, who set off on a series
of adventures involving lots of happy discoveries and coincidences.
The tale, written in the 18th century by the author Horace Walpole,
is called 'The Three Princes of Serendip', in which Serendip is
an old name for the island country of Sri Lanka.

In the course of their journey, the princes found themselves following
the tracks of a camel that they had been wrongly accused of stealing.
Through a combination of luck and careful attention, as well as
following clues such as the patches of grass the camel grazed at and
the imprints it left in the ground, they were able to tell that the animal
was limping, blind in one eye, missing a tooth, carrying a pregnant
woman, and holding honey on one side and butter on the other!
Through more episodes of luck and good fortune, the story
had a happy ending – the princes were welcomed into the
kingdom's royal palace and enjoyed a successful life.

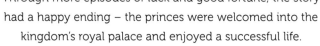

The author Horace Walpole invented the word
'serendipity' to describe the three princes' adventures.
To this day, thanks to the story of Serendip, 'serendipity'
means the making of happy and unexpected discoveries.

EBULLIENT

Bubbles blown with washing-up liquid.

Bubbles foaming at the top of a bath.

Bubbles fizzing away in a drink.

People have embraced the joy of bubbles for centuries.

The Romans knew bubbles as *bulla*, while to boil water was known as *ebullire*. From these beginnings, English took the word 'ebullient', which means cheerful and lively, as though we are 'bubbling up' or 'fizzing' with energy. In fact, when someone has a very lively and fun personality, we can also describe them as 'bubbly'!

IRIDESCENT

In the ancient legends of the Greeks and Romans, Iris was
the goddess of the rainbow, as well as a messenger for the gods.
People believed that every rainbow was a bridge or road that
had been let down from heaven and was used as a path for Iris
to carry her messages. For the Greeks and the Romans, 'iris'
itself became the word for 'rainbow'.

Today, we use 'iris' for the coloured part of our eyes – blue,
brown, or green – the part with the black dot of the pupil at its
centre. It was given the name 'iris' because of its variety of colours.

Iris can also be found within the beautiful word 'iridescent',
an adjective that describes objects that gradually change colour
when seen from different angles. When you look at a soap bubble
in the light, you can see its many colours. Seashells and butterfly
wings are also iridescent; they shimmer with the
colours of the rainbow.

DUMBLEDORE

All Harry Potter fans will recognize the word
'dumbledore', used as the name of the headmaster of
Hogwarts, a school for young witches and wizards. What
you might not know is that the word 'dumbledore' existed
for hundreds of years before this wise headmaster
appeared, and it meant something quite surprising –
though some would say just as magical.

In dictionaries of the 18th century, you would find
'dumbledore' described as a 'bumblebee'. These precious
insects are crucial to the environment because they take
pollen from one plant to another so that new ones can grow.
Bumblebees help us produce vegetables, plants and many
other crops, and their distinctive drone or buzz is a familiar
and welcome sound of summer. 'Dumbledore' is made up of
'dumble', which sounds like a humming or buzzing insect,
and 'dore', an old word for the insect itself.

PLODGE

Is there anything more freeing than jumping in puddles, and hearing the joyous splashes and sploshes of wellington boots as they land in the tiny pools of water? Many of us love the squelch of mud too: the soft and sticky sound as we try to make our way across boggy land on a wet and wintery day.

English has a word for plunging into water or wading across muddy ground: plodging. The very sound of 'plodge' creates a picture in the mind of soft or swampy ground. As for the mud, there is another very old local word for this, too, which is 'clart'. So the next time you try to wade across muddy, squelchy earth, you can happily say you are 'plodging through the clart'!

QUIDDLE

To quiddle is to make yourself busy with little
things as a way of avoiding the important ones.
There are many words in the dictionary and
thesaurus that express the same idea of
pottering about or wasting time. Some from the
past include 'picking a salad', 'spuddling',
'dawdling', 'slummocking' and 'moodling'.

SOSS

This 200-year-old verb means to fall
with a thud on to something soft.

It describes the pleasure of

flopping into a comfy armchair

and staying there.

SMEUSE

If you've ever spotted a small hole in a hedge
or at the bottom of a fence, you may not know
that you are looking at a 'smeuse', an opening that
allows the passage of animals such as rabbits and
hares. The word is a blend of the words 'meuse',
meaning a hiding place, and 'smoot', meaning
a small hole or opening. If you crouch down
to peer through a smeuse, you never
know what you might see!

SNOODGE

Is there anything nicer than a morning without an alarm set, when you can simply pull the covers over your head and snuggle as long as you like? The dictionary is full of words for nestling cosily in this way. One of them is 'snoodging', which means making yourself comfortably warm and sheltered.

You could also say you are 'snuzzling', 'snoozling', 'croozling', or 'snoodling'. Have you noticed most of these all start with the letters 'sn-'? Perhaps there is something in their sound that suggests making ourselves cosy and snug?

HURKLE-DURKLE

Hurkle-durkling, an expression from 19th-century Scotland, is something most of us are guilty of doing sometimes – it means lounging about in bed long after it's time to get up! If you are a hurkle-durkler, you might also be a 'yawmagorp', a 200-year-old word for a person who yawns and stretches all day long!

'Hurkle-durkle' is an example of the many fun, cheerful expressions in English that contain two words with similar and often rhyming sounds. You might like going on a helter-skelter at a funfair, or wearing flip-flops while playing ping-pong and eating a KitKat!

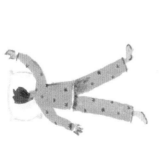

NIDIFICATE

Feathers and moss, small twigs and woven grass –
these are all things that a bird might collect when
building its nest, to ensure a soft, smooth and cosy
home for its chicks to hatch in. Have you ever
been lucky enough to see a nest up close?
If so, you might have noticed how intricately
it has been designed and put together.

When birds make nests, they are 'nidificating',
a word that comes from the Latin *nidus*, 'nest'.
Humans have an impulse to nidificate too –
perhaps not with grass and twigs, but by
making a cosy den in which to snuggle.

CRUMP

Many words in our language sound
very much like the thing they are describing.

Imagine something PLOPPING into water,

for example,

or the PITTER-PATTER of raindrops,

the TICK-TOCK of a clock,

the DING-DONG of a doorbell,

or the HISS of a snake.

Words like these use 'onomatopoeia' (pronounced
ono-mato-pee-uh), where they copy the sound of the thing
they describe. Another of these is 'crump' – if you say it out
loud, perhaps you can imagine how it is used? Picture a
field of deep, firm snow, and the noise your boots might
make as you walk across it. That is crumping!

SUSURRUS

Imagine an autumn day, and you've stepped outside,
closed your eyes and tuned into the lovely sounds around
you. You might notice the soft rustling of leaves in the breeze.
Or, if you're on a beach, you might hear the mesmerizing
murmur of waves rolling into the shore from the sea. There is
a word for such beautiful, soothing sounds: 'susurration',
which comes from the Latin *susurrus*, meaning 'whisper'.
It's a lovely idea – that the water or leaves are
whispering to you from afar.

LOVELIGHT

To feel loved is a precious gift. We experience love in the
way people behave, but often we can also see it written on
their faces and expressions. We once had a special word for the
radiant look of love in a person's eyes: 'lovelight'. If you're ever
feeling blue, think about someone who you look upon with
'lovelight', and see if that brings some joy to your day.

THUNDERPLUMP

We have all experienced a thunderplump, even if we didn't know there was a name for it! This is the sudden downpour of fat, heavy raindrops that leaves us drenched and dripping in minutes. The word 'plump' has been used to describe a downpour in the Scots language for over 300 years. If that downpour is accompanied by rumbles of thunder, or if it is so heavy that it batters roofs and beats down on umbrellas with a mighty roar, then it is a 'thunderplump'.

The dictionary doesn't record the use of the word as a verb – at least not yet – but wouldn't it be wonderful if, when we've been caught in the rain and arrive home soaked to the skin, we could bring a little light to the dark, dreary day by declaring, 'I've just been thunderplumped!'?

DARDLEDUMDUE

Do you know someone who walks through life with their head in the clouds, lost in their imagination and not always noticing what is happening around them? These people are daydreamers, a word that has described those who regularly drift off into pleasant thoughts for over 300 years.

In the local vocabulary of East Anglia, there was once another name for a daydreamer: 'dardledumdue'. The term might conjure up a picture of a happy country-dweller ambling along a country lane while singing a tuneless 'dumdeedumdue' tune. But does something else come to your imagination when you hear the word 'dardledumdue'? Perhaps that is part of the beauty of the word – that it can conjure up so many different images, and really mean whatever we want it to!

YAKAMOZ

Have you ever been lucky enough to see the ocean
at night, when the Moon shines down upon it and gives
it an enchanting sparkle? English has no single word for
the glittering flashes of light that bounce off the sea as
the waves roll under the night's sky. But the language of
Turkish does – 'yakamoz' is the magical reflection of
moonlight upon the surface of the sea.

Something so delightful should surely have
a name, wherever you are in the world.
Perhaps we could bring 'yakamoz'
to the English language?

CLINKABELL

Along with 'cocklebell' and
'conkerbell', 'clinkabell' is an
old word for an icicle.

CONKER

Is there anything more fun than kicking
through a deep layer of autumn leaves and finding a
shiny conker peeking out among them? These seeds of
the horse-chestnut tree, with their deep, mahogany shine, are
something to be marvelled at. You might have threaded them
with a piece of string and challenged your friends to a game
of conkers? But where does their name come from?

The word 'conker' probably began with a word for 'snail shell',
known as a 'conch', because snail shells were first used to play the
game. The word quickly became associated with 'conqueror', which
went on to become another name for the knockout contest. Playing
conkers became so popular that people created lots of words for the
different sizes, colours and categories of conker. A new conker is
called a 'none-er' because it hasn't yet conquered any other
conkers – the player must say 'addy addy onker' to christen it.
As soon as it does break another it becomes a 'one-er',
then a 'two-er', and on it goes. And if the strings become
entangled, the first player to shout 'stringsies' has an
extra turn. Victories are known as 'kingers'!

GIGGLEMUG

A gigglemug is someone who
is constantly smiling.

CHORTLE

'"O frabjous day! Callooh! Callay!" he chortled in his joy.'

To 'chortle' is to chuckle in a noisy and gleeful way.
Its inventor was Lewis Carroll, who used it in his nonsense poem
The Jabberwocky. Carroll loved making up new words by taking
parts of existing ones and putting them together in new ways.
'Chortle' is a mixture of 'chuckle' and 'snort' – a perfect combination
for a guffaw – you can almost hear laughter in its sound.

Today we call such word mashups 'blends', but Lewis Carroll gave
them the name 'portmanteau', an old word for a suitcase, because
he saw them as two parts folded together to make one.

Is there someone in your life who always
makes you chortle?

SNOTTINGER

Victorian slang for a handkerchief.

RETROUVAILLES

Imagine two lovers reuniting at the end of a film, or families hugging at the airport after a long time apart. Many of us have experienced the sadness of being away from family and friends. How much sweeter is it when you see them again after a very long time? The French have a single word for the happiness we feel when we are reunited with someone we love – 'retrouvailles'. It comes from *retrouver*, meaning 'to find again', because when we experience the joy of 'retrouvailles' with a person we have greatly missed, we are celebrating finding them again.

SHIVELIGHT

'Shivelights and shadowtackle
in long lashes lace, lance and pair.'

Can you picture yourself in a dense forest,
looking up at the canopy of trees above?
Now and then, you might see a lance of
light shining through the leaves, casting a
shadow on the ground beneath you.

For the poet Gerard Manley Hopkins, writing a
century and a half ago, this was known as 'shive-light':
slivers or splinters of light that break through the
treetops. Hopkins also invented the word
'shadowtackle', meaning a latticework of
shadows reflected on the forest floor.

SCURRYFUNGE

To scurryfunge is to rush around, trying
to tidy up before guests arrive.

BLUTTERBUNGED

Some things in life can cause great surprise and shock.
From the sound of a balloon popping, to a birthday
party you hadn't expected, or a present you never
thought you'd receive, some surprises are
definitely better than others.

In all cases, though, an unexpected event can
leave you totally 'blutterbunged'. This is an old word
from Lincolnshire meaning 'dumbfounded' or
'overtaken by surprise'. The word neatly suggests an
inability to talk or move because you are so taken
aback. While it's not always a pleasant feeling, there's
a certain joy that comes from telling people you
feel truly and utterly blutterbunged!

GONGOOZLER

On a warm summer's day, there are few nicer things
to do than sit lazily on the bank of a river or canal and watch
the world go by. The activity on the water can be mesmerizing,
as boats chug past and navigate bridges or bends. A word was
born a hundred years ago to describe someone who loves
to watch this kind of activity – 'gongoozler'.

Gongoozlers like nothing better than sitting and watching
other people being busy on a canal or river. Their name is
probably based upon an old British word: 'gawn', meaning
to 'stare lazily at something'. Which means that if you
like staring for a long time out of the window, or at
other people or at anything at all, you can call
yourself a gongoozler too!

SUPERCALIFRAGILISTIC

It's hard not to start singing when you hear
'supercalifragilisticexpialidocious', one of the longest words
to have ever made it into the dictionary. It is a fun invention
that first began to appear in the 1930s, and was then made
very popular by the Disney film *Mary Poppins* in 1964.

'Supercalifragilisticexpialidocious' is used to express
excitement and approval, a little like 'fabulous!' or 'fantastic!'
but with added zing. Even though the film's song states that
'the sound of it is really quite atrocious', its bouncy, rhythmic
sound is very hard to resist. So next time you're impressed
or amazed by something, you know what to say!

EXPIALIDOCIOUS

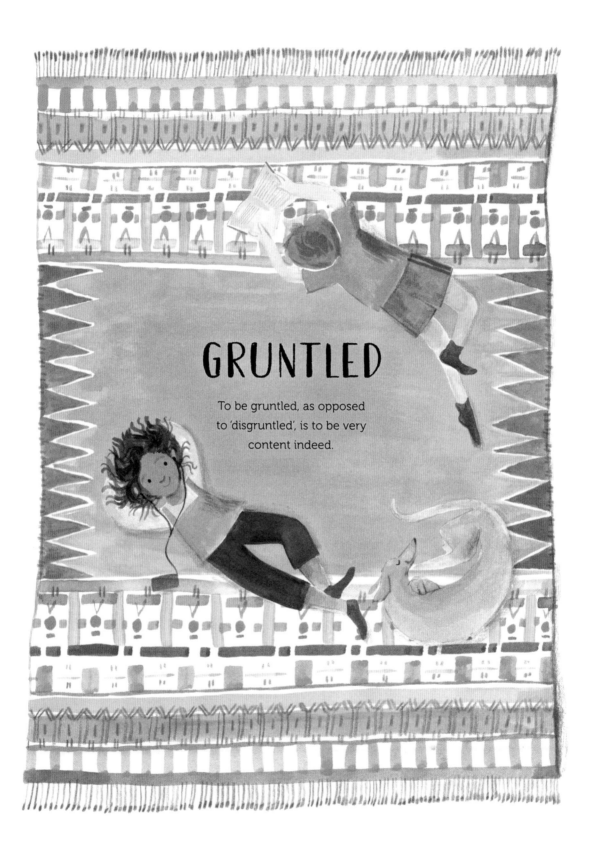

GRUNTLED

To be gruntled, as opposed to 'disgruntled', is to be very content indeed.

KVELL

Do you feel a little embarrassed when someone boasts about your achievements to other people? Although it might make us feel a bit uncomfortable, usually this is done because they are proud and happy for you! There is a particular name for this kind of gushing – 'kvelling'. It comes from the language of Yiddish, traditionally spoken by central and eastern European Jews and their descendants. Yiddish took a lot of words from German, and 'kvell' comes from the German *quellen*, meaning 'to well up'. Which means that anyone kvelling about the success of someone they love is positively welling up with pride!

You might recognize other words from Yiddish too – including 'bagel', 'glitch' (an error) and 'schlep' (to drag oneself).

BOFFOLA

Smiling – even when we fake it – sends signals to our brain to make us feel happy. And laughing does the same thing, which means both have an extraordinary power to lift our mood! This is why we all love a good joke, because a funny one makes us smile and a *really* funny one makes us laugh out loud! One word for an uproariously funny joke that produces peals of laughter is a 'boffola', which is based on 'boffo', meaning a loud and hearty guffaw. 'Boffola' also conjures up the sound of a laugh rumbling up from your stomach, don't you think?

'Laughter is the best medicine.'

EUCATASTROPHE

A eucatastrophe is the opposite
of a 'catastrophe' and means
a happy ending.

GROAK

Have you ever sat down to enjoy a biscuit or
piece of toast, only to see your dog gazing up at you
longingly? Or perhaps you find yourself craving a
chip or two from your friend's plate as they eat? If
you recognize these situations, you already know all
about groaking. This word from English dialect means
staring intently at someone in the hope that they
might share their food. Dogs groak extremely well,
but humans can be pretty good at it too!

PETRICHOR

After a long period of dry, hot weather, when it feels
as though the Sun has been beating down relentlessly, the rain that
follows is often highly welcome and anticipated. You can almost smell
its arrival in the air, and imagine the pitter-patter of the droplets
pelting against the ground before they've even fallen.

After such a downpour, the ground gives off the unmistakable scent of
fresh rain. This scent has a name, which was coined in the 1960s by
two scientists who discovered it is made by a mixture of substances
that collect on the ground. They called the distinctive, earthy
smell of rain after warm and dry weather 'petrichor'. It has a
beautiful story behind it, as it is made up of 'petr-', meaning
'rock', and 'ichor', which in Ancient Greek myth was
a fluid believed to flow through the veins of the
gods. The idea is of something magical and
mysterious, just like the scent itself.

STARTLER

Do you like using exclamation marks?!!!!! We have been using them for more than 500 years. This excitable punctuation mark may come from a Latin word *io*, meaning 'joy', which was made into a symbol of an upper case I with the 'o' as a tiny dot below it.

There have been many nicknames for the exclamation mark over the centuries – including 'startler', 'wonderer', 'gasper', 'screamer', 'pling' and 'boing'. But perhaps beware of adding too many 'startlers' to your writing – the author Terry Pratchett once said, 'And all those exclamation marks, you notice? Five? A sure sign of someone who wears his underpants on his head'!!!!!

YOLO

There are lots of words in English, and particularly in English slang, that are written as a series of letters. Some of them are what we call 'abbreviations' – a.m., for example, means morning because it is short for the Latin *ante meridiem*, 'before midday'. Others are pronounced as though they are words in themselves, and are known as 'acronyms'. 'Scuba', for example, is actually an acronym for 'self-contained underwater breathing apparatus'.

YOLO is another, more modern acronym, which stands for 'You Only Live Once'. It is used particularly on social media to mean that you should go ahead and do something silly or even slightly dangerous because you may never have the chance again. It encourages us to live life to the full, because we only get one chance. So why don't we leave our worries about the past and future behind, and embrace the idea of YOLO!

FIRGUN

'Firgun' is a very joyful thing, for it means the selfless pleasure we feel when someone we love succeeds. The word comes from Hebrew and describes a heartfelt generosity and true positivity. There is even an International Firgun Day, celebrated each year on 17 July, when we are encouraged to share compliments and congratulate others on their achievements. Perhaps every day should be a Firgun Day, when we do our very best to let people know how special they are?

BESTIE

Our besties are our very best friends,
with whom we share good days and bad.

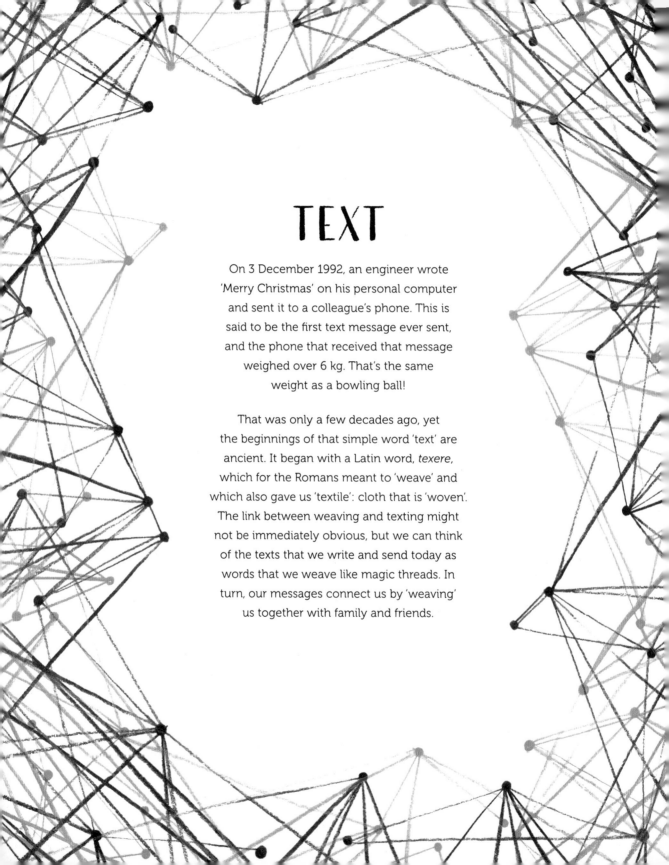

TEXT

On 3 December 1992, an engineer wrote 'Merry Christmas' on his personal computer and sent it to a colleague's phone. This is said to be the first text message ever sent, and the phone that received that message weighed over 6 kg. That's the same weight as a bowling ball!

That was only a few decades ago, yet the beginnings of that simple word 'text' are ancient. It began with a Latin word, *texere*, which for the Romans meant to 'weave' and which also gave us 'textile': cloth that is 'woven'. The link between weaving and texting might not be immediately obvious, but we can think of the texts that we write and send today as words that we weave like magic threads. In turn, our messages connect us by 'weaving' us together with family and friends.

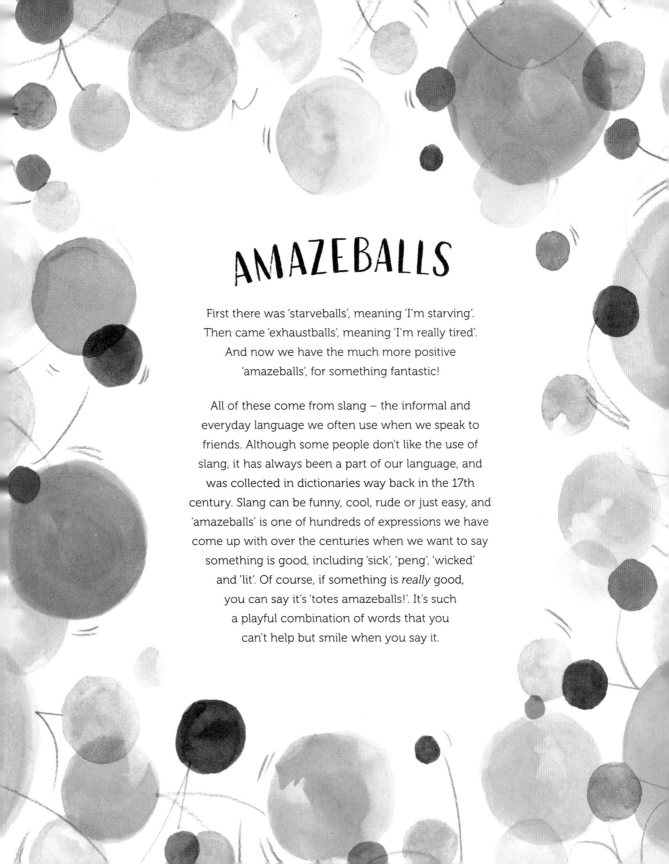

AMAZEBALLS

First there was 'starveballs', meaning 'I'm starving'.
Then came 'exhaustballs', meaning 'I'm really tired'.
And now we have the much more positive
'amazeballs', for something fantastic!

All of these come from slang – the informal and
everyday language we often use when we speak to
friends. Although some people don't like the use of
slang, it has always been a part of our language, and
was collected in dictionaries way back in the 17th
century. Slang can be funny, cool, rude or just easy, and
'amazeballs' is one of hundreds of expressions we have
come up with over the centuries when we want to say
something is good, including 'sick', 'peng', 'wicked'
and 'lit'. Of course, if something is *really* good,
you can say it's 'totes amazeballs!'. It's such
a playful combination of words that you
can't help but smile when you say it.

EMOJI

Emojis are tiny images each showing different emotions or objects, from a face crying with laughter, or two people hugging, to flags from every corner of the globe. Their story began in the 1980s, when typists began to show emotions using keyboard characters, such as :) for a smile. These were known as 'emoticons', short for 'emotion icons'. A decade later, new pictorial images were created on computers, and were given the name 'emojis'. This word comes from the Japanese words *e*, meaning 'picture', and *moji*, meaning 'letter' or 'character'.

Emojis are the fastest moving area of language, but some people argue that emojis are not real language and must never replace it. While words are always important, the Ancient Egyptians used a writing system based on pictures known as 'hieroglyphs'. These often featured animals – a gecko, for example, was used to mean 'many' because the Egyptians would have seen them everywhere. An angry-looking baboon was used to show anger. History tells us that language and communicating can be much broader than simply using words.

GIGIL

A kitten peeking out from under a blanket; a puppy nuzzling
the camera lens; a baby's first smile – we might find these
incredibly cute moments so adorable that we want to give
the person or animal a cuddle! In the language of Tagalog,
spoken in the island country of the Philippines in the western
Pacific Ocean, there is a word for wanting to squeeze
something or somebody tight because they are just so cute!
The word is 'gigil', which sounds a little bit like 'giggle', and
describes a sudden outburst of affection. If you've ever
had someone in your family squeeze your cheeks out
of pride or joy, you will know all about 'gigil'!

SNACCIDENT

A snaccident is the accidental eating
of a lot of snacks when you meant
to have just the one.

NEFELIBATA

It's a lovely image – the idea of being so caught up in your thoughts that your head is lost in the sky. That is the meaning of the Portuguese *nefelibata*, which describes someone who loves to live in their imagination. Its literal meaning is 'one who walks in the clouds'.

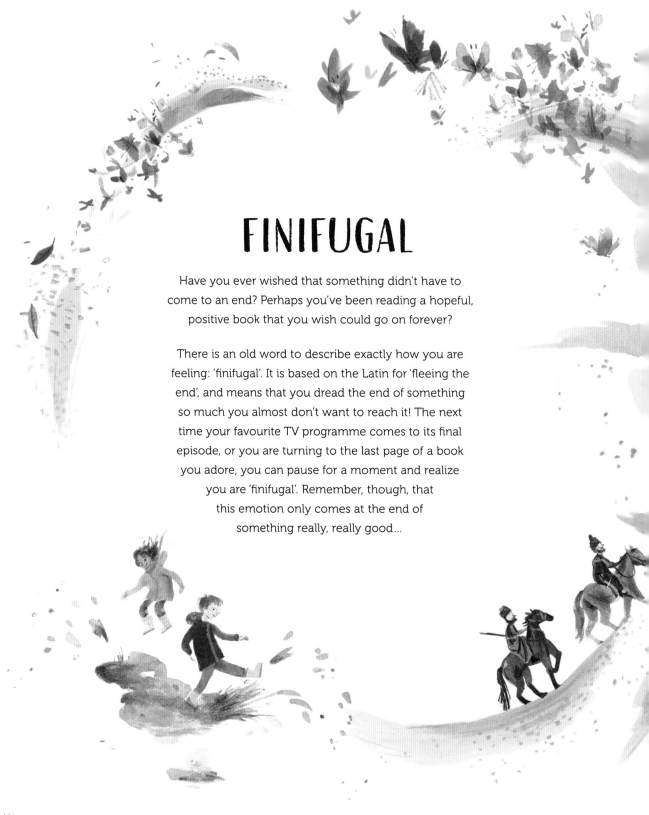

FINIFUGAL

Have you ever wished that something didn't have to come to an end? Perhaps you've been reading a hopeful, positive book that you wish could go on forever?

There is an old word to describe exactly how you are feeling: 'finifugal'. It is based on the Latin for 'fleeing the end', and means that you dread the end of something so much you almost don't want to reach it! The next time your favourite TV programme comes to its final episode, or you are turning to the last page of a book you adore, you can pause for a moment and realize you are 'finifugal'. Remember, though, that this emotion only comes at the end of something really, really good…

PRONUNCIATION GUIDE

Amazeballs
[amaze-balls]

Apricity
[apr-iss-ity]

Aurora
[or-roar-a]

Bellycheer
[belly-cheer]

Bestie
[bes-tee]

Blutterbunged
[blutt-er-bunged]

Boffola
[boff-o-la]

Butterfly
[butter-fly]

Cacklefart
[cack-ell-fart]

Cerulean
[suh-rule-ee-uhn]

Charm
[char-m]

Cheer
[ch-eer]

Chortle
[chaw-tle]

Clinkabell
[clink-a-bell]

Confelicity
[con-feliss-itee]

Conker
[conk-er]

Cordial
[cor-dee-ull]

Crump
[krump]

Cwtch
[kuch]

Dardledumdue
[dar-duhl-dum-doo]

Darling
[dah-ling]

Dewlap
[dew-lap]

Dimpsy
[dimps-ee]

Dog
[dog]

Dormouse
[door-mouse]

Dumbledore
[dum-bul-door]

Ebullient
[e-bull-ee-unt]

Elixir
[elix-ear]

Emoji
[emo-gee]

Erumpent
[e-rump-uhnt]

Eucatastrophe
[yew-catas-trofee]

Fellowfeeling
[Fellow-feeling]

Finifugal
[finny-foo-gul]

Firgun
[feer-gun]

Fizzle
[fizz-ull]

Flother
[flo-ther]

Forblissed
[for-blissed]

Freond-spedig
[fray-ond sped-ich]

Friended
[frend-ed]

Gigglemug
[giggle-mug]

Gigil
[gig-il]

Glamour
[glam-er]

Gongoozler
[gon-gooz-luhr]

Good
[gud]

Gorm
[gawm]

Gossamer
[goss-a-mer]

Groak
[grohk]

Gruntled
[grunt-uld]

Halcyon
[hal-see-on]

Happify
[happee-fy]

Happy
[hap-pee]

Hibernacle
[hi-burr-nack-ell]

Hurkle-durkle
[her-kel-der-kel]

Inwit
[in-wit]

Iridescent
[ir-ee-de-scent]

Kitten
[kitt-en]

Kvell
[k-vell]

Lagom
[la-gom]

Lick into shape
[lik in-to shayp]

Lovelight
[love-light]

Lovewende
[love-wen-der]

Lullaby
[lulla-bye]

Matutinal
[ma-toot-in-ull]

Meander
[mee-ander]

Mellifluous
[mel-iff-loo-uss]

Mubble-fubbles
[mubbel-fubbels]

Muscle
[muss-uhl]

Nefelibata
[neh-fell-ee-barta]

Nidificate
[nid-if-i-kate]

Niveous
[nivv-ee-us]

Panacea
[pan-uh-see-uh]

Petrichor
[pet-ree-kor]

Plodge
[plodj]

Quiddle
[quid-ell]

Respair
[ruh-spare]

Retrouvailles
[ruh-troov-i-yuh]

Ruth
[rooth]

Scintillate
[sin-till-ate]

Scurryfunge
[scurry-funj]

Seijaku
[say-yak-u]

Serendipity
[ser-uhn-dip-itee]

Shivelight
[shy-ve-light]

Smeuse
[smews]

Snaccident
[snacks-i-dent]

Snoodge
[snoo-dj]

Snottinger
[snot-in-jer]

Soss
[soss]

Spindrift
[spin-drift]

Startler
[start-ler]

Supercalifragilisticexpialidocious
[super-cala-fra-jill-is-tick-ex-pee-ally-doe-shus]

Suspire
[suss-pire]

Susurrus
[suss-er-uhs]

Text
[tex-t]

Thunderplump
[thunder-plump]

Tickle
[tik-uhl]

Tree
[tree]

Vermicelli
[ver-mi-chell-ee]

Yakamoz
[yak-a-moz]

YOLO
[yo-low]

Zephyr
[zeffer]

I'm grateful to the wonderful team at Puffin Books
for inspiring me to look on the bright side of language:
to Phoebe Jascourt for her enthusiasm and wisdom in
commissioning the idea, Sarah Connelly for managing the
project so effortlessly, and for Katy Finch, Arabella Jones,
Sally Griffin and Becky Hydon for making *Roots of Happiness*
look and feel so special. And, of course, huge admiration and
thanks go to Harriet Hobday, who has worked her magic to
make my favourite words sparkle from every page.